Crystals & Creativity: practical steps to embrace your inner artist

Pia Tohveri PhD

ISBN-13: 978-1533642738
ISBN-10: 1533642737

Contents

Introduction:

Crystal love for the soul

A journey of crystals and creativity

During this journey of crystals and creativity you will explore the artist within you and awaken a curiosity about who you are and what you can create. You will get to know crystals that can help you to unravel, focus and expand your creativity. Through working with crystals you will find that there is so much more to your creativity than you knew. You will release stagnation, unblock your creative source and discover new ways of looking at your art. At the end of the journey you will have learnt to support your creativity through honouring and nourishing it in your own unique way.

Materials

To do this creative journey, you will need the following materials. Fifteen crystals, detailed below, a journal and/or sketchbook and art materials to create the practical work in the exercises. To ensure that you will get the most out of this creative journey, you will work in your own chosen medium, such as acrylic, pen, ink, watercolour, oil, collage, photography or mixed media. There are no size restrictions to the art you will create, the choice is yours.

A circle of crystals for your journey

Crystals

The crystals that you will work with in this book are the following:

Rose quartz
Black tourmaline
Smoky quartz
Clear quartz
Citrine
Amethyst
Aventurine
Carnelian
Lapis lazuli
Rutilated quartz
Aquamarine
Sugilite
Sodalite
Watermelon tourmaline
White agate

Crystal care

Cleanse your crystals before and after using them to keep their energies fresh and vibrant. This can be done by washing the crystals in water, passing them through the smoke of sage or Palo Santo, using Tingsha bells or burying them in soil for a few hours. If you are attuned to Reiki you can also use the power symbol to cleanse the crystals. Please note there are a crystals that should not be washed in water, such as selenite and halite, as they will disintegrate. We are not using these crystals in this journey but for future reference please look up the crystal if you are unsure.

Keep your crystals in a dedicated place when you are not using them, such as a box, basket or drawer. You may want to store the crystals in a box with compartments and label these to keep the crystals organised. Or you might want to keep them in a special pouch made of silk or velvet.

Be kind to your crystals and they will continue to inspire you on your journey of creativity.

Let's begin the journey.

Chapter 1

Crystal creations

The creativity process and crystals

When we create, we tap into the spark of the divine
within us. The ideas that emerge make us feel in tune
with our soul, and we become blissful. Creativity can
be expressed in many different ways, through
painting, writing, photography, drawing, music and
movement, each with their own specific way of
expression. The uniqueness of our soul's imagery
comes alive through these mediums. Sometimes
creativity becomes stagnant and we feel blocked and
can't progress further. Or we might feel that we have
come to a point on our artistic path where we want
to change direction but we do not know how to
proceed. Sometimes we may feel that there are new
ideas lying under the surface but they have not yet
sprung forth and they need unlocking. Crystals can
motivate us to find new ways of creating by clearing
blocks and revealing innovative ideas. By working
together with crystals, you can open up and receive
your inner creative wisdom and expand this into the
world.

Crystals work their magic in many ways, and their energy can be perceived in varying degrees of subtle to very powerful. As part of energy medicine and healing, crystals cleanse, activate and balance chakras and other points on the body. This process aligns the body, mind and soul and makes us feel complete. Some people are more sensitive than others to crystals, and they can immediately feel the substance or value of the crystal. While others are more affected by the colour of crystals and the sensory quality of wearing them. You don't have to believe in crystal healing to use the crystals in this book, they are chosen to assist you in making creative progress and simultaneously opening up the true you.

Meditating with the crystals

In each chapter of the book, there are sections for meditating with the crystals. What this means is that you will spend time connecting with the crystals and attuning to their energies to get to know them. You will open up a dialogue with the crystal which might be visual or textual, and after the meditation you will be asked to make notes and draw about your experience. To enhance your meditative space, you can burn incense and play your favourite relaxation music. The meditation time can range from 5 to 15 minutes, follow your own guidance to the length, and note that this might vary according to the different crystals. By relaxing and allowing your body to respond to the crystal energies you will feel a deeper connection to the crystals and understand how they can support you in embracing your creativity. This on-going meditative practice will enable the flow of ideas from your own creative source and release any blocks that are holding you back.

Crystals and the chakras

During the meditations, you will be asked to place the crystals on the different chakras on your body. Chakras are situated at specific points on our bodies through which energy flows. Healthy chakras emit energy that flow in a balanced manner and they have a reciprocal relationship with the other chakras. Blocked or weak chakras cause imbalance and can affect the overall well-being of a person. The chakras are associated with colours, elements, physical, emotional and spiritual issues.

Earth Chakra

The earth chakra is located below the feet and governs our connection to the earth and our ability to be grounded in who we really are.

Associated colour: black

Root Chakra

The root chakra is located at the base of the spine. It governs basic survival issues regarding food, money, social position, and how supported we feel in the world.

Associated colour: red

Sacral Chakra

The sacral chakra is located at the lower abdomen, two inches below the navel and two inches in. This chakra governs emotions, abundance, sensuality, pleasure and sexuality.

Associated colour: orange

Solar Plexus Chakra

The solar plexus chakra is located in the upper abdomen in the stomach area. It governs self-worth, confidence, will, inner power and self-esteem.

Associated colour: yellow

Heart Chakra

The heart chakra is located at the heart. It governs intimacy, balance, relationships and the ability to receive and give love.

Associated colour: green or pink

Higher Heart Chakra

The higher heart chakra is located at the sternum. It is the gateway to the heart and governs compassion and unconditional love.

Associated colour: turquoise

Throat Chakra

The throat chakra is located at the throat. It governs communication, expression, creativity and speaking our truth.

Associated colour: blue

Third Eye Chakra

The third eye chakra is located at the forehead between the eyes. It governs intuition, imagination, wisdom, dreams, inner vision and the ability to make decisions.

Associated colour: indigo

Crown Chakra

The crown chakra is located at the very top of the head. It governs consciousness, understanding, thoughts and our connection to the divine and pure bliss.

Associated colour: violet and white

Chapter 2

Love, ground and cleanse

Beginning with love

Self-love is the foundation to our own being, the very basic building block that creates and makes us honour who we are. Sometimes limited beliefs about ourselves can create false scenarios which make us forget our loving character. Emotional traumas may have prevented access to our inner love-fountain and we have gradually forgotten that it exists. We are often self-critical and don't express enough love for who we are. Through focusing on self-love, we are able to open up to a new sense of self-acceptance. This process can connect us to aspects of the creative soul that lie dormant in the heart space. In this chapter we will love, ground and cleanse ourselves with three crystals, rose quartz, black tourmaline and smoky quartz.

Rose quartz, black tourmaline and smoky quartz

Rose quartz

The soothing beautiful pink rose quartz is all about love and compassion. It helps to open our heart chakra so that we can receive and send out love. Rose quartz increases sensitivity and empathy and helps us to be gentler to ourselves and makes us feel more connected to other people. It reminds us to forgive ourselves and others. The soft vibration of rose quartz can heal many emotional traumas and heart centred issues. It can be perceived as a 'best friend' crystal that you can communicate with about your worries and knowing it will support you.

Rose quartz will support your creativity with compassion and it will emphasise that what you create is originating from a place of love.

Meditation to connect with rose quartz

Lie down for this meditation.

Hold the rose quartz in your hands for a few minutes.

Place the rose quartz on your heart chakra.

Take a few deep breaths and relax.

Stay in meditation for 5 to 15 minutes.

After the meditation, write and draw/paint in your sketchbook about the below questions:

What is creativity for you?

Why would you like to be more creative?

How does it feel when you create, are you calm, elevated, aligned?

Grounding and letting go of any blocks

The beautiful love and healing you received from rose quartz provided the foundation for your creative journey. To take your creativity further, we will examine how to be grounded and remove blocks that you may have in your body, mind or soul that prevent you from moving forward. To be grounded and fully present in the body enables you to focus on your projects and ensure that nothing will stand in the way of your expression. Removing blocks will prepare you to take artistic ideas forward with innovation and you will feel more freedom in your creativity

Black tourmaline

Black tourmaline is an opaque black crystal with a calming and grounding energy. It will help you to connect with the earth and to focus and commit to your soul-call. It can establish a link with your ancestors and cleanse your family line. Black tourmaline is protective and it will always ensure that you are safe. It can be used to create a grid in your office or home to keep it safe from negative energies.

In creating art, black tourmaline will make you feel grounded and focused and help you to commit to your projects.

Smoky quartz

Smoky quartz has a grey transparent colour and a glassy surface, and resonates with the energy of letting go. It will help you to release blocks that prevent you from going forward. Smoky quartz is relaxing and can relieve physical pain. It can help to release issues of the shadow-self that are lodged deep inside and therefore bring forth a new level of understanding of who you are.

Smoky quartz will help you to loosen up your creative blocks and limited self-beliefs so that you can connect with your own vision and explore your ideas in new ways.

Connecting with black tourmaline and smoky quartz

For this meditation please lie down in a comfortable place.

Place the black tourmaline below your feet, your earth chakra.

Place the smoky quartz on your root chakra.

Take a few deep breaths and relax.

Stay in meditation for 5 to 15 minutes.

After the meditation, write and draw/paint in your sketchbook about the below questions:

Do you feel grounded after the meditation?

Did you release any blocks to your creativity, if so, what did you release?

Did you receive any guidance on how to proceed on your path as an artist?

Colour, crystals and art making

When working with crystals and the colour palette in creating art, our attraction to a particular colour may be directly influenced by its' healing vibration, as applied in colour therapy. Different colours may influence our well-being through their respective wavelengths and enhance our moods and correct physical imbalances. The practical application of colour when creating art allows for an additional healing possibility. Different mediums, such as paint, ink and pastels, enable us to experience colour as a tactile sensation which can unblock new ways of creating.

Take a few minutes to consider how colours affect you and then journal about the below questions:

Do you prefer blue or red tones?

How does it feel when you see extremely bright colours?

How does the texture of your chosen art medium, oils, acrylics, inks, pastels, make you feel?

What is your favourite colour and how does it make you feel?

An altar of love and power

Create an altar of love and power

To explore the feelings of love and power, your
assignment will be to create an *altar* that reflects these
values. An altar is a space where you can display
items that are sacred to you. Your altar can be used
for prayers, wishes and act as a material space for
manifesting your dreams and desires. Choose objects

that you feel comfortable and resonate with, and place these on the altar to represent your intentions.

You will be prompted to create a new altar for each chapter. You may want to leave the current altar in its' place until it is time to change it. Or you may only wish to build your altar as a temporary ceremonial space and dismantle it after the exercise.

Use your rose quartz, black tourmaline and smoky quartz, together with images and objects to create an altar that represent love and power for you. You can use flowers, candles, herbs, cards, photos or any other objects when you create your altar.

When you feel your altar is complete, step back and look at it.

Then sit down in front of your altar and meditate to connect with the energy of love and power.

Stay in meditation for 5 to 15 minutes.

After the meditation, journal about the following questions:

What does love mean to you?

How does it feel to be in love and loved?

How do you express love? Are you verbal, tactile or do you show your love by doing things?

How does it feel to be in the energy of power?

In which aspect of your life do you feel that you lack power?

What areas of your life are empowered?

Empowering Art

Based on your meditations, journal and sketchbook exercises with rose quartz, black tourmaline and smoky quartz, your project is to create a piece of art that represents love and power. Consider the different qualities of rose quartz, black tourmaline and smoky quartz and see if you can capture their essence in your art. Remember you are free to use any medium you want and there are no size restrictions.

Keep your rose quartz, black tourmaline and smoky quartz close to your art space so that you can tune into their energies and let them guide you in the process. If you wish you can start the art making session by making a grid of grounding, empowerment and self-love. Place the crystals on your table where you keep your art materials and put the black tourmaline, smoky quartz and rose quartz in a triangle formation. Put the crystal you feel most attracted to at the closest point to you. Then start creating your art piece and tune into the feeling of love and power.

When you feel you have come to a natural stopping point, take a step back from your art. Look at what you have created and feel inside yourself if your piece of art makes you feel loved and empowered. Try to sense how your art piece wants to grow further and how you can take it to the next level, and then continue creating.

If you feel you lose focus at any point during the creative process, please take a moment and pause from what you are creating. Hold the rose quartz in your hand for a moment, then the black tourmaline and then the smoky quartz. This will re-connect you with the crystals and their support in enhancing your creative spirit.

Remember that you are in charge of what you create and you can change it at any time.

Be empowered and create with love.

Chapter 3

Open up and receive

Cleansing and creativity

The previous chapter gave you a grounding journey of love and empowerment to start the process of exploring your creative soul. Now we will cleanse blocks, open up the inner spark and start to consider the joyful essence of our own creativity. After we cleanse ourselves we will gradually become more receptive and able to access more of the creative essence which we hold inside. In energy healing, the term cleansing refers to the clearing of stagnant energy from the chakras and auras and other areas of the body that may be clogged with outworn ideas, repetitive thoughts and emotional wounding. Cleansing away debris from a person's energetic field will make the energy clear and open up the possibility to receive new ideas, inspiration and forge a focused path ahead.

Clear quartz and citrine

Clear quartz

Clear quartz is a wonderful cleanser and amplifier of healing. It emits power, clarity and the essence of pure spirit. The transparency of clear quartz is used by healers in Central America as a directional object to locate illness in the body. Australian Aborigines use it in healing ceremonies to heal the body and soul. Clear quartz spheres have been used in divination in the Western world and are a familiar tool in a psychic reader's tool kit. Clear quartz has a high energetic vibration that cleanses and cuts away clogged energy in chakras. It changes the mood in spaces by bringing in clarity, focus and spiritual energy. If anything else fails, I use clear quartz to cleanse and heal.

For creativity, clear quartz provides clarity as it cleanses stuck debris from all chakras. It will heighten your focus and provide a clean slate for new ideas to manifest.

Connecting with clear quartz

Sit or lie down for this meditation.

Place the clear quartz on your solar plexus.

Take a few deep breaths and relax.

Stay in meditation for 5 to 15 minutes.

After the meditation, write and draw/paint in your sketchbook about the below questions:

How did the clear quartz cleanse make you feel?

Do you feel like you released something significant?

Did you receive any messages of clarity?

Citrine

Citrine is radiating abundance with an invigorating orange colour that sparkles with joy. It is cleansing and energising and brings happiness into your life. Citrine balances and stimulates all the chakras so that they align with a refreshed energy. It attracts prosperity when placed in the abundance corner in the home according to the Feng Shui Bagua map.

When using citrine for creativity, it brings joy to the process of making things and it makes your own ideas flow with sparkling energy.

Connecting with citrine

Sit or lie down for this meditation.

Place the citrine on your sacral chakra.

Take a few deep breaths and relax.

Stay in meditation for 5 to 15 minutes.

After the meditation, write and draw/paint in your sketchbook about the below questions:

Do you feel more balanced and energised after the meditation?

Did you get any insights to which chakra you could work more with?

Did you receive any messages of creativity?

Allowing joy to rule

When we are in the vibration of receptivity we feel more joy in our bodies and we can progress smoothly along our creative path. Clear quartz can cleanse away old doubts and stubborn debris, while citrine can help you to feel energised and spark new ideas. Consider how you allow yourself to receive joy in your life and how this impacts on your creativity. Then do the following meditation.

Sit in a comfortable position.

Hold the clear quartz in your right hand and the citrine in your left hand.

Ground yourself and take a deep breath.

Stay in meditation for 5 to 15 minutes.

After the meditation, journal about the below questions:

Do you feel joy when you think about starting a new project?

Is there anything that prevents you from moving forward that you would like to cleanse?

How do you see the process of cleansing and receiving helping you further in creating art?

An altar of receptivity

Create an altar to receive

Use your citrine and clear quartz to create an altar of receptivity. Place any images, tarot cards, plants, candles, flowers or objects that you feel resonate with you being open to receiving.

When you feel your altar is ready, step back and observe what you have created.

Sit down by your altar and meditate on the feeling of receptivity.

Stay in meditation for 5 to 15 minutes.

After the meditation, journal about the following questions:

How does it feel to be open to receiving?

Is there anything that you feel has not been brought to the surface?

How can you become more receptive?

Receptivity and joy

You are now ready to explore your sense of
receptivity and joy through creating a piece of art
that makes you feel more open to welcoming new
ideas. Consider how you experienced clear quartz and
citrine, and see if you can emulate this in material
form. Recall how clear quartz and citrine cleansed
stagnant energy and allowed you to open up in a
joyful way to receiving what is best for you.

Keep your clear quartz and citrine close to your art
making space to stay connected to their energies. You
can open up the art making session by cleansing and
energising the room in the following way. Hold the
clear quartz in your hand and sweep the room in an
anti-clock wise direction to cleanse the space. Then
hold the citrine and sweep the room in a clock-wise
direction to bring in the feeling of joy.

If there is a specific colour that you feel resonates
with the vibration of receptivity and joy use this as
your starting point. You might want to use orange as
the opening colour as it is associated with the sacral
chakra and the ability to receive. Go further and be
brave as you experiment with your sense of
receptivity and joy through layers of colour.

Step back from your art piece at regular intervals and
observe if your art reflects how you feel about

receptivity and joy. If you feel disconnected at any time, take a pause and hold the clear quartz for a few minutes in your hand to re-connect with its' energy, and then repeat with the citrine. Trust your receptive intuition as you progress with your creation.

Create from your inner joy and stay in the sparkling light.

Chapter 4

Getting into the flow

Accessing your gratitude

To flow with the creativity that lies within enables us to access many levels of information. This can occur as a spontaneous rush of ideas appearing with an urgency and we may find ourselves drawing and writing in our sketchbooks for hours. Or this could be a longer process where small pieces of ideas reveal themselves slowly to us over time. Your own divine ideas combine parts of your soul, your truth, your inner world and how solid the connection between these aspects are. Crystals can help to increase the flow of creativity by connecting you to gratitude and accessing the spiritual dimensions of your inner voice.

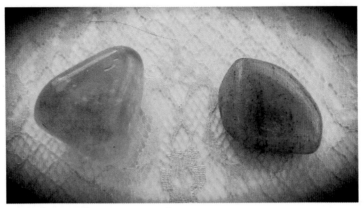

Amethyst and green aventurine

Amethyst

Amethyst is an enlightening and awakening crystal. It deepens our connection to the divine and heals regrets and sorrow. Amethyst has a delightful purple colour and it has been highly valued throughout history as a stone of royalty. It connects you to your inner Zen and emphasises spiritual awareness. Amethyst is useful for dream work and for transmuting obstacles when connecting to our higher self.

In creativity, amethyst opens up the spiritual connection with your art. It can help to heal any traumas and disappointments you have experienced when creating art in the past and makes you trust your highest vision.

Connecting with amethyst

Lie down in a comfortable place.

Place the amethyst on your crown chakra.

Take a few deep breaths and relax.

Stay in meditation for 5 to 15 minutes.

After the meditation, write and draw/paint in your sketchbook about the below questions:

How did you feel connecting with amethyst?

Did you get any messages from your artist higher-self?

Did you connect to the spiritual aspects of your creative mission?

Green aventurine

The sparkling beauty of green aventurine works wonderfully with the heart chakra. It has a lush vibration of abundance and expansion and it also brings balance. Green aventurine helps to open up your heart and to connect the dots in your emotional journey with gratitude. It can be simultaneously gentle and strong as it connects you with what needs to be released or healed. Green aventurine helps to overcome heart break when you have decided it is time to truly move on.

For creativity, green aventurine synchronises your heart with your creative flow and infuses a sense of trust that you are on the right path.

Connecting with green aventurine

Lie down in a comfortable place.

Place the green aventurine on your heart chakra.

Take a few deep breaths and relax.

Stay in meditation for 5 to 15 minutes.

After the meditation, write and draw/paint in your sketchbook about the below questions:

How did you feel connecting to green aventurine?

Did you receive any guidance to increase your creative flow?

Did you meet your gratitude guide?

Nature loves gratitude

Spending time in nature is an inspirational way to connect to the flow of gratitude. The cycles of the different seasons and the patterns of germination, growth, harvest and decay of plants, trees and flowers can help us to connect to our bodily rhythm and to find our inner place of gratitude. Women's sensitive and sensual bodies often empathise with the lunar energies and the ebb and flow of the moon's cycles. Connecting to nature's changeable presence and experiencing the earth's bounty can help us to access new levels of gratitude.

For this exercise, bring your amethyst and your green aventurine and go outside in nature and find a place which feels special to you. This can be a place that you already know or a brand new place that you will discover along your walk. When you have found your sacred place, look around the area and soak in the beauty of your surroundings and choose a comfortable place to sit down.

Take a few moments to ground yourself and let your mind be quietened and tune into the flow of the earth.

Hold your amethyst in your left hand and your green aventurine in your right hand.

Stay in meditation for 5 to 15 minutes.

After the meditation, journal about the below questions:

How does it feel when you see the colours of nature around you?

Do you sense energies when you connect to the trees, flowers and plants around you?

If you could be a specific tree, flower or plant, which one would you choose and why?

An altar of balance

Create an altar of balance

To proceed on the path of creativity your assignment
is to create an altar of balance. Place your amethyst
and green aventurine on your altar. Put images, oracle
cards, candles, flowers, plants or any other objects
that you feel represent balance for you on the altar.

Sit by your altar and look at what you have created.

Close your eyes and meditate on the feeling of balance.

Stay in meditation for 5 to 15 minutes.

After the meditation, journal about the following questions:

In which areas of your life would you like to create more balance?

How could you create more balance in these areas?

How could you use your art to create more balance in your life?

The flow and gratitude of art

Start creating a piece of art that embodies flow and gratitude. This could be developing a sketch that you have drawn after the meditations with amethyst and green aventurine. Or you might want to go ahead and start fresh with a new idea. Keep your amethyst and green aventurine close to your art space and explore the feelings of flow and gratitude. Feel how the crystals are connecting your crown and heart chakra and making you aware of your creative flow.

If you feel disconnected at any time, step back from what you are creating. Hold your amethyst in your hand for a few minutes to tune in with its' energy and then repeat with your green aventurine.

Remember that being in the present moment and creating with gratitude opens up a flow of ideas and an awakening of the potential you hold inside.

Enjoy the flow and experience of gratitude in creating.

Chapter 5

Creating from the heart

Create heart art

A balanced heart ignites creativity to emerge in innovative ways and softens our approach to that which we create. When we are truly synchronised with our heart space, the creation of art becomes a profound experience. The energy field of the heart has been measured by science and it expands far beyond the physical body itself. It has been suggested that the heart as a thinking organism helps us to make decisions, to forgive and to move on. In this chapter, we will go deep into our heart space and connect with our true self by exploring forgiveness. Deep emotions may arise as we work from our heart space, embrace these and know that you are ready to take the steps and move on to embracing your true being.

Rutilated quartz and aquamarine

Rutilated quartz

Rutilated quartz contains pieces of rutile, golden coloured strands of titanium oxide that resemble angel or fairy wings. It aligns the chakras, making our metaphorical wings grow and prepares us for expansion. Rutilated quartz helps to manifest what is the best for us. It is excellent for journey work as it connects to the angelic realm and shows possibilities that we have not been brave enough to envision. Rutilated quartz brings in light and elevates the mood when life feels draining.

In creativity, rutilated quartz can make you change direction and embrace a whole new way of creating.

You may also feel called to using metallic and sparkling paints and art materials.

Connecting with rutilated quartz

Lie down in a comfortable place.

Place the rutilated quartz on your third eye chakra.

Take a few deep breaths and relax.

Stay in meditation for 5 to 15 minutes.

After the meditation, write and draw/paint in your sketchbook about the below questions:

How did you feel connecting with rutilated quartz?

Was there a spark that was alighted anywhere in your body?

Did you experience the golden light of the rutiles?

Aquamarine

Aquamarine is a delicate pale turquoise crystal with a soft flowing energy that is nurturing, soothing and relaxing. Aquamarine's gentle ambience is full of truthfulness and it brings a calm sensation of well-being through its' watery connotation. It is named *aqua marina* from the Latin seawater and sailors made protective amulets depicting Poseidon from aquamarine to keep them safe in their journeys.

Aquamarine helps us to evaluate our creativity by slowing everything down and asks us to observe our art from a balanced and honest perspective.

Connecting with aquamarine

Lie down for this meditation.

Place the aquamarine on your higher heart chakra.

Take a few breaths and relax.

Stay in meditation for 5 to 15 minutes.

After the meditation, write and draw/paint in your sketchbook about the below questions:

How did you feel connecting to aquamarine?

Did you sense any watery imagery?

Did you get an image or message of the art that wants to be created?

Forgiveness

Forgiveness is a powerful process in the healing of the heart. By accepting past hurts and releasing these we can find balance and be open to exploring new ways to create from our heart space. If we do not forgive ourselves and/or others, we might end up carrying resentment which can prevent us from being fully aware of our creative gifts. Rutilated quartz helps us to forgive ourselves and others by raising our vibration through its' golden like strands, while aquamarine supports our highest truth and inner knowing. Consider how forgiveness could help you to move on in your life and on your artistic path. Then do the below meditation.

Sit down in a comfortable place.

Hold the rutilated quartz in your right hand and the aquamarine in your left hand.

Close your eyes, take a few deep breaths and tune into your heart.

Stay in meditation for 5 to 15 minutes.

After the meditation, journal about the following questions:

Is there somebody you need to forgive?

Is there something you have not forgiven yourself for?

If any strong emotions come up during this process, please allow these feelings to flow through you. Cry and release any stagnation and feel old hurts leaving you. Ground yourself by stamping your feet and bring awareness to your whole body. Know that you are bringing out a new you through this process.

An altar of new beginnings

Create an altar of new beginnings

Consider how a new beginning could be materialised
for you and how this would make you feel. Put your
rutilated quartz and aquamarine on your altar. Place
any other images, candles, flowers, plants and objects
that represent new beginnings for you, together with
the crystals.

Spend a few minutes looking at your altar and observe the imagery.

Then sit down in front of your altar and meditate on a new beginning.

Stay in meditation for 5 to 15 minutes.

After the meditation, journal about the following questions:

What would a new beginning mean to you?

How does your heart chakra feel at the moment?

What steps will you take to create a new phase in life?

Heart Art

Start creating a piece of art that truly resonates with your heart space. Consider the qualities of rutilated quartz and aquamarine, let them guide you and go deep into your heart space and explore how you can expand your creativity to new levels. You might feel drawn to using a different set of colours than before. You might want to use a different medium, or change the size you usually work in. Let your heart space take you on a journey and be open to new avenues of creativity.

Before you begin creating your art, take a few moments and settle your mind in quiet contemplation. Feel the love in your heart space and envision it radiating through your whole body. Know that you are always enough and there is no need to pretend to be somebody else. Feel inspired, connect with the angelic realm and be one with your heart.

Keep the rutilated quartz and aquamarine close to your art space and tune into them from time to time. Allow yourself to change anything in your art as your progress in the session.

If you feel unfocused at any point, step back from your art piece and ground yourself. Then hold your rutilated quartz for a few minutes in your hand and tune into its' energy, and then do the same with aquamarine.

Thank you for being brave this week and creating from your heart.

Chapter 6

The Muse is calling – will you answer?

What is my calling?

When we experience the true bliss of passionate creation, we open up boundaries and let ourselves loose. In this chapter we will explore the essence of the muse and how this sparks creativity. Historically, a muse is a person that ignites passion and inspires artists to create art. We will expand the boundaries and consider the essence of the muse as a passionate trigger for creating art. By acknowledging the inspiration of an external source and how they awaken sensations in us, we can access a whole new level of creative ideas.

Carnelian and lapis lazuli

Carnelian

Carnelian's striking orange red colour increases warmth and raises energy by cleansing blocks to intuition. It enhances sexuality and sensuality and makes us feel more in tune with our female side. Carnelian nurtures the inner child and balances fears of expression. It cleanses any self-limiting beliefs of being too modest and not being able to embrace our true self. It is a real healer of women's issues and it is empowering, nurturing, cleansing and balancing.

In creativity, carnelian awakens our inner child and ignites our passion and links these with our unique ideas, sometimes in a surprising way.

Connecting with carnelian

Lie down for this meditation.

Place the carnelian on your sacral chakra.

Take a few deep breaths and relax.

Stay in meditation for 5 to 15 minutes.

After the meditation, write and draw/paint in your sketchbook about the below questions:

How did you feel connecting to carnelian?

Did you meet your creative guardian Goddess?

Did you get any messages for your sacral chakra?

Lapis lazuli

Lapis lazuli is a gorgeous blue colour with golden veins through it. It has a wise, empowering vibration full of strength and helps us to rise above problems by solving them in a grounded way. Lapis lazuli helps us to move forward and to trust our own power. It is supportive and makes us develop our negative traits in a constructive way.

Lapis lazuli helps to bring out the utmost in your creativity by making you courageous to trust your own strengths and focusing on these.

Connecting with lapis lazuli

Lie down in a comfortable position.

Place the lapis lazuli on your throat chakra.

Take a few deep breaths and relax.

Stay in meditation for 5 to15 minutes.

After the meditation, write and draw/paint in your sketchbook about the below questions:

How did you feel connecting with lapis lazuli?

Did you receive any messages of how to go forward in your creativity?

Did you sense a creative guardian spirit?

Creative union

I invite you to explore your creativity further by meditating on the connection of your female and male sides of the body. Our brains have a right and left hemisphere and we classify the right side as female and the left side as male. The left, male side of the brain, governs the right side of the body, while the right, female side of the brain is in charge of the left side of the body.

The male side is connected to logic, rationality, linear thinking, and understanding. The female side is connected to caring, feelings, emotions, nurturing, compassion and love. In creativity, our artistic expression can reach new levels when we unite our female and male sides and we can start creating from a more balanced perspective.

In this meditation we will work with the sacral and throat chakras to form a bridge between our female and male sides. The sacral and throat chakras link us to our creativity and expression, and by connecting them we can bring forth deep and unique ideas.

Lie down for this meditation.

Place the carnelian on your sacral chakra and the lapis lazuli on your throat chakra.

Take a few deep breaths and tune into your sacral and throat chakras for a few minutes.

Then put the carnelian on your throat chakra and the lapis lazuli on your sacral chakra.

Take a few deep breaths and tune into your sacral and throat chakras for a few minutes.

You can do this meditation when you feel the need to balance your female and male side.

After the meditation, write and draw/paint in your sketchbook about how you experienced the Creative Union meditation.

An altar of passion

Create an altar of passion

To further connect with the artistic spark within you,
your assignment will be to create an altar of passion.
Place the carnelian, lapis lazuli and also rose quartz

on your altar. Find any other images, flowers, candles, cards and objects that represent passion for you and incorporate these into the altar.

Consider how the colours and imagery of the altar awaken passion in you.

Sit by your altar and meditate on the feeling of passion.

Stay in meditation for 5 to 15 minutes.

After the meditation, journal about the following questions:

What does it mean for you to be passionate?

Who or what makes you feel passionate?

Have you experienced heightened passion when creating art, how did this feel?

Art Musings

Who is your muse? Have you encountered a muse that awakened such passion inside you that you had to create something? Muses arrive at various times during our lives and in many different shapes. In this exercise we expand the classical notion of the woman as a muse and explore the energy of the muse not only as a person, but also as an object, plant, flower, animal or place.

Consider your most awesome muse and how they made you feel. Focus on how you can create a piece of art that embodies the passion you felt when encountering them.

Keep the carnelian and lapis lazuli close to your art space to connect to their energies. Recall the meditation of the creative union and how the different qualities of carnelian and lapis lazuli complement each other energetically to bridge your female and male sides.

You could experiment with complementary colours and observe if your muse will materialise in a shape that you recognise. Or perhaps start creating with your eyes closed to connect to the spark of the muse. Feel free and let the energy of your passion guide you as you create.

If you feel disconnected at any time, please step away from your art and ground yourself. Hold the carnelian in your hand for a few minutes, and then the lapis lazuli, to re-connect to their vibration.

Be in passion and create with your muse.

Chapter 7

Seek and transform

Embracing the creative self

Is it good or bad? Self-criticism might be the toughest aspect in an artist's journey. Looking at your own creations with an objective eye can feel overwhelming. We might feel that we are not good enough to create art and get stuck in patterns of constantly comparing ourselves to others. This can make us fall into self-doubt and we might hide behind obstacles which we cannot see past. Creating art is an incredibly personal and intimate process. There is no wrong way to create and to be open to the possibilities of seeing beyond what we create is a powerful process. Learning how to handle criticism can be revelatory. By facing our fears and detaching from these we begin to trust our own voice. To help us move forward on the creative journey, we will look deeper at ourselves by working with the concept of transformation. This will help us to come to an understanding of what it is that we really want to say to the world with our art.

Sodalite and sugilite

Sodalite

Sodalite is a deep dark blue crystal with a calming energy and it helps us to find our own truth. It has a grounding effect which can be perceived as dreamy. Sodalite can take us on a deep journey inwards to explore hidden parts of our creative self. It is excellent for de-stressing and for slowing down a hectic pace of life. Sodalite can help us to meet our inner-self from a non-critical perspective.

For creativity, sodalite helps to consolidate ideas with patience and makes us step out of our comfort zone with a new, more confident view on ourselves and our art.

Connecting with sodalite

Lie down for this meditation.

Place the sodalite on your solar plexus.

Take a few deep breaths and relax.

Stay in meditation for 5 to15 minutes.

After the meditation, write and draw/paint in your sketchbook about the below questions:

How did you feel connecting to sodalite?

Did you meet your inner critic?

Does it make you feel empowered knowing that you have full control over your own artistic path?

Sugilite

Sugilite has a magical deep purple colour and vibrates with a transformative energy of nurture and love. It allows the body and soul to expand in a sensory way and heightens all the senses, helping us to experience the world more fully. Sugilite might feel elusive to start with, but once a connection has been made, it will open up and give us many new levels of understanding.

Sugilite helps to connect our creativity to the soul's wishes and it can enhance our mystical vision when creating art. It helps to bring out the deeper aspects of creativity that have been hiding inside our soul.

Connecting with sugilite

Lie down for this meditation.

Place the sugilite on your heart chakra.

Take a few deep breaths and relax.

Stay in meditation for 5 to 15 minutes.

After the meditation, write and draw/paint in your sketchbook about the below questions:

How did you feel connecting with sugilite?

Did the purple light feel stronger in any part of your body?

Did you meet your inner mystical artist?

Fire release for detachment

It can be difficult to stay objective to our own art as we have a personal and emotional involvement with it. By stepping outside of ourselves and detaching from that which we create, we can view our art objectively. This might make us more aware of what we need to work on to progress. Begin to consider detachment and what you can let go of to evolve as an artist. You might want to detach from being too critical of your art. Or maybe you have not been able to proceed as you feel stuck working in a specific style that you don't feel connected to any more. Perhaps you have been too self-conscious to arrange an exhibition. By detaching and looking at our art with objectivity, we can transform and find new ways to take our art further.

For this meditation, sit down in a comfortable position.

Take a deep breath and ground yourself.

Hold the sodalite in your right hand and the sugilite in your left hand for a few moments.

Contemplate on what you wish to detach from on your artistic path.

Write these down on a piece of paper.

Fold the paper and sit with it between your hands and feel that all that is no longer needed is leaving you and creating space for transformation.

Shred the paper into small pieces and place these in a fire proof container and set them on fire. Watch and feel your obstacles being transformed as they burn and transform into smoke.

An altar of transformation

Create an altar of transformation

Place the sodalite and sugilite on your altar together with images, oracle cards, plants, flowers and objects that represent transformation for you. You could incorporate cards with words to represent the transformative state of where you want to be. Or if you wish, you can place your own art on, or close to, the altar to instigate a process of artistic transformation.

Sit in front of your altar and meditate on the feeling of transformation.

Stay in meditation for 5 to 15 minutes.

After the meditation, journal on the below questions:

How does the essence of transformation feel to you?

Do you feel anything needing to shift for you to be able to move forward?

What do you feel would be the greatest gift of transformation?

Transformational Art

Working through this chapter might have surfaced feelings of intense transformation and the realisation that you are fully in charge of the process of creating your art. By tuning into the supportiveness of sodalite and sugilite you will feel a new confidence in releasing and transforming your creativity. You might feel that your art style calls for completely new imagery. Feel free to paint over a piece of art that you are not happy with to explore the concept of transformation and observe the new imagery emerging.

Keep the sodalite and sugilite close to your art space, and tune into their vibration and let them support you as you experiment with new shapes, materials and forms. Remember that when you start to transform your art, this will parallel your soul's call to transform what is not working for you anymore in your life.

If you feel stuck at any time, take a break and step back from what you are creating. Hold your sodalite in your hand for a few minutes to re-connect with its' energies, and then repeat with your sugilite.

Transform and be bold, you got this.

Chapter 8

The art is your oyster

Connecting with your art and healing yourself

Our own art often holds the secret to who we truly are and this can provide clues to what lies next on our creative journey. By connecting to the essence of our own art, it is possible to expand the vision held inside and bringing this out into the world. In this last chapter, we will explore our own being through making a self-portrait. Exposing yourself in material form can be seen as an act of bravery as you create a version of you that feels immensely truthful. Facing your own physical form and aligning this with your soul's call can bring life-changing revelations.

Watermelon tourmaline and white agate

Watermelon tourmaline

Watermelon tourmaline is a mesmerising colour of green and pink and has an active, connective and expansive energy. It stimulates the heart chakra and helps to unite all the chakras, making us feel complete. Watermelon tourmaline breaks through pre-conceived ideas and patterns and helps us to feel more universally connected. It promotes movement of the body, such as yoga and dance, and can help to boost the flow of creativity as experienced through the body.

In creativity, watermelon tourmaline supports our fearlessness in experimenting with shape and form. It helps us to connect to our source and create what we feel truly passionate about.

Connecting with watermelon tourmaline

Lie down for this meditation.

Place the watermelon tourmaline on your sacral chakra.

Take a deep breath and relax.

Stay in meditation for 5 to 15 minutes.

After the meditation, write and draw/paint in your sketchbook about the below questions:

How did you feel connecting to watermelon tourmaline?

Do you feel more connected to the world around you?

Did you receive any messages of how to connect with creativity through your body?

White agate

White agate has a beautiful lustrous colour of white and it brings calmness and peace. It transmutes stubborn and heavy patterns and makes our whole being peaceful. It reveals who we really are by purifying and heightening spiritual awareness. White agate helps to align the body, mind and soul with its' true purpose.

For creativity, white agate unveils a path of spiritual illumination and makes us more tranquil when exploring new ways of making art.

Connecting with white agate

Lie down for this meditation.

Place the white agate on your heart.

Take a deep breath and relax.

Stay in meditation for 5 to 15 minutes.

After the meditation, write and draw/paint in your sketchbook about the below questions:

How did you feel connecting to white agate?

Did you feel that your body, mind and soul are linked at a higher level?

Did you receive any insights of your true essence?

Meditating with your art

To explore the true you and what you have learnt about yourself so far, I invite you to do a meditation to connect with your own art. You can repeat this meditation as often as you want. It will enable you to communicate with your art in an intimate setting and reveal new ways to access ideas and inspiration for your future projects.

Gather the art you have created in this journey and place them around you.

Sit down in a comfortable position and look at all the incredible things you have made.

Close your eyes and ground yourself.

Connect with the energy of your art pieces.

Meditate on the energy of your art for 5 to 15 minutes.

After the meditation, journal about the below questions:

Is there a piece or art that you are particularly proud of and why?

How does it make you feel when you look at it?

Is there anything you feel that you could have done better?

An altar of you

Create an altar of you

Place all the crystals that you have worked with in this creative journey on your altar. Put any other cards, objects, flowers, plants, candles and images that you feel represent the true you on the altar. In addition, you can place a photograph of yourself that you really love on the altar. You can also place the art pieces you have created on this journey around your altar.

Use this final altar as a meditative reflection of what you have achieved during this journey. Take a photo of the altar and save it as a pictorial reference to remind yourself of what you have created and how much you have evolved. It can also be used as a visual grounding point to remind you what direction you wish your art to progress in the future.

Sit in front of your altar and meditate on its' energy.

Tune into your own being and appreciate who you are.

Stay in meditation for 5 to 15 minutes.

After the meditation, journal about the below questions:

How does it feel to be surrounded by material representations of the true you?

Does the altar awaken something in you? Happiness, sadness, relief?

Self-portrait

For your last exercise you will create a self-portrait that reflects the true you. This process will help you to complete the journey that you have taken so far and it will prepare you for the next step. By creating a material representation of yourself you will reinforce what you have learnt and this will build confidence in yourself as well as in your art projects.

To help you to connect to your own true being, do the below meditation.

Lie down and place the amethyst on your crown chakra, white agate on your third eye, aquamarine on your throat chakra, rose quartz on your heart, lapis lazuli on your solar plexus, watermelon tourmaline on your sacral chakra, carnelian on your root chakra and the black tourmaline by your feet, the earth chakra.

Take a few deep breaths and relax.

Stay in meditation for 5 to 15 minutes.

After the meditation, consider the below questions:

Do you feel you have changed working with crystals?

Does your heart-art space feel more open?

Is there anything specific you want to focus on after this journey?

Start creating your self-portrait

The self-portrait can be done in a realistic or abstract style, in your preferred medium. Be open to any new insights when creating your portrait. You have all the tools you need to bring out your vision, trust the process and create from your inner art space. Keep your watermelon tourmaline and white agate close to your art space and connect with them before you start making your first marks. Experiment with colour and form, flow with your soul's desire and see your own image emerging.

If you run into any blocks while creating your self-portrait, take a break and step back from your art. Ground yourself and hold the watermelon tourmaline in your hand for a few moments to re-connect with its' energy, and then repeat with the white agate.

Remember that you are truly unique and your gifts are waiting to be shared with the world.

Celebrate with crystal love

You have gone through a journey of self-discovery, taking your creativity to new levels by getting to know crystals that helped you further on your artistic path. This process has opened up new ways of expressing and experiencing your creativity. The most important aspect is that you listened to your own soul, created from your heart space and opened up to your own unique vision. From this point onwards you will step ahead and embrace the true artist you are.

Give yourself a big hug and celebrate.

About the author

Pia Tohveri, PhD, is an artist, writer, healer and anthropologist. She believes in everyday magic, finds immense joy in crystals and moon bathes at every possible occasion.

Made in the USA
Columbia, SC
01 December 2022

72138029R00051